SPEED MACHINES

MUSTANG

Julia J. Quinlan

PowerKiDS
press.

New York

Published in 2013 by The Rosen Publishing Group, Inc.
29 East 21st Street, New York, NY 10010

First Edition

Editor: Jennifer Way
Book Design: Greg Tucker

Photo Credits: Cover Paul Stringer/Shutterstock.com; p. 4 6th Gear Advertising/Shutterstock.com; pp. 5, 18, 19 DDCoral/ Shutterstock.com; p. 6 Omikron/Photo Researchers/Getty Images; p. 7 © www.iStockphoto.com/Peter Mah; p. 8 Shamleen/ Shutterstock.com; p. 9 John Olson/Time & Life Images/Getty Images; pp. 10, 24 © Hans Dieter Seufert/c/age fotostock; p. 11, 29 Bloomberg/Getty Images; pp. 12–13, 25, 28 Darren Brode/Shutterstock.com; p. 14 esbobeldijk/Shutterstock.com; p. 15 Naiyyer/Shutterstock.com; p. 16 Gary Whitton/Shutterstock.com; p. 17 Barry Blackburn/Shutterstock.com; p. 20 © Ken Brown/flickr; p. 21 (top) © Glenn Hall/flickr; p. 21 (bottom) jenskramer/flickr; p. 22 Jeff Kowalsky/AFP/Getty Images; p. 23 Getty Images News/Getty Images; pp. 26–27 Mirco Lazzari/Getty Images.

Library of Congress Cataloging-in-Publication Data

Quinlan, Julia J.
  Mustang / by Julia J. Quinlan. — 1st ed.
      p. cm. — (Speed machines)
  Includes index.
  ISBN 978-1-4488-7459-0 (library binding) — ISBN 978-1-4488-7531-3 (pbk.) —
  ISBN 978-1-4488-7606-8 (6-pack)
  1. Mustang automobile—Juvenile literature. I. Title.
  TL215.M8Q56 2013
  629.222'2—dc23
                                    2012004836

Manufactured in the United States of America

CPSIA Compliance Information: Batch #B4S12PK: For Further Information contact Rosen Publishing, New York, New York at 1-800-237-9932

Contents

The Original Pony Car

Mustangs are all-American muscle cars. They are not as rare or as expensive as European sports cars, such as Lamborghinis. Mustangs are fast, powerful, and **innovative**, though. This means that Mustangs are made using the newest ideas in car making. In fact, the first Ford Mustang changed the world of sports cars

The latest Mustangs are always popular at car shows. Here is one at the North American International Auto Show, in Detroit, Michigan, in 2009.

Classic, or older, Mustangs are popular with people who collect sports cars. Owners show them off at classic car shows like the one shown here.

completely! This Mustang was the first "pony car." Pony cars are sports cars that have seats in the back. Most sports cars only have two seats in the front. Pony cars are also small and light compared to other sports cars.

The first Mustang was introduced in 1965. Ford hoped to sell 100,000 Mustangs in that first year. It sold 22,000 in the first day! After 18 months, it sold 1 million Mustangs! As of 2012, more than 9 million Mustangs have been sold! People love the Mustang because it is a cool-looking, powerful car that is also **affordable**.

The Ford Motor Company

The Mustang is designed and **manufactured** by the Ford Motor Company. Ford is one of the most successful American carmakers in history. Henry Ford started the company in 1903. Ford has made many notable cars. One of these was the Model T, which was first made in 1908. The Model T was the first car made with affordability in mind. Before the Model T, only wealthy people could afford to own a car. The Model T was in production until 1928, and almost 16 million were sold!

Here are workers on one of Ford's early assembly lines. Being able to make more cars at a faster rate was one way Ford was able to sell them at a lower cost.

By 1918, half of all cars in the United States were Model Ts.

Ford was also the first company to have an automobile **assembly line**. It began using assembly lines in 1913. Having an assembly line made making cars faster and easier. Today, almost all cars are made on an assembly line. Ford has been making leaps in technology and business since 1903. One of its biggest leaps was the invention of the pony car, with the Ford Mustang.

American Power

The Mustang was introduced at a time when the leading sports cars came from European companies, such as Alfa Romeo and Ferrari. Two Ford employees, Lee Iacocca and Donald Frey, came up with the idea of a pony car. They decided that the new Ford sports car would need to have a back seat. The idea of adding a back seat seems simple now, but at the time no other company was doing that.

This mid-1960s Mustang is famous for its high-performance engine called the Windsor engine.

Here Lee Iacocca poses with a Mustang.

By having a back seat, the Mustang became much more practical than the European two-seaters, with their small trunks. It is sporty and fun, but there is room in the back for more passengers. There is also a large trunk for groceries and luggage. The Mustang was so successful that almost every other American carmaker had its own version of a pony car by 1967.

Customized Mustangs

One of the things that car owners like the most about Mustangs is how **customizable** they are. This means owners can choose among several options for many of the car's parts. Mustangs come in many different colors. They can have different wheels and different lights. They can also be hardtops or convertibles. Today's Mustangs can even have glass roofs so drivers and passengers can look up and see the sky!

This owner of this Mustang GT has chosen a coupe, or hardtop, with a black paint job.

Here is the engine of a 2008 Shelby Mustang GT-C. This is a higher-performance version of the Mustang with an engine built by the Shelby American car company.

Modern Mustangs have either V6 or V8 engines. The engine is called a V engine because it is shaped like a V. The number after the *V* tells you how many **cylinders** the engine has. The more cylinders an engine has the more powerful it is. Most cars have fewer than six cylinders. There are 11 different models of Mustangs being made as of 2012. All 11 models have many different options. These options allow each car owner to have exactly the car he wants.

Turnkey Racers

Many car companies make racecars. Racecars are different from sports cars and not meant for everyday driving. Companies like to make racecars because it shows how great their cars can be and how good they are at **engineering** powerful cars.

Ford makes a series of **turnkey** Mustang racecars. "Turnkey" means that racing teams can order a Mustang racing car that is ready to be driven without having to make changes to the body or the engine. These cars are made to be raced in a number of different race series. For example, the 2012 Boss 302R is made to be raced in the Grand-Am Continental Tire Sports Challenge. The 2012 Boss 302S is made for track racing and road racing. The 2013 Cobra Jet is made for drag racing. One of the most successful racing cars was the FR500C. It won the Grand-Am **Championships** in 2005, 2008, and 2009.

Here is a 2012 Mustang Boss 302. The Boss Mustangs are higher performing than other Mustangs. The 302S and 302R are the racing versions.

Many Kinds of Racing

When the Mustang was first introduced in the 1960s, most American automakers did not have racing teams. However, Ford raced the Mustang in the 1964 Tour de France international rally and won! Since then, Mustangs have competed in many different races. Some teams drive Mustangs in the National Association for Stock Car Auto Racing, or NASCAR.

Here is a Mustang FR500 racing in the Total 24 Hours of Spa endurance race, in Belgium. An endurance race tests a car and its driver's performance over a long period.

Here is a Mustang being worked on by a pit crew in a 2011 race in Dubai, United Arab Emirates.

NASCAR is the most popular racing series in the United States. A stock car is a racecar that is based on an existing production car.

Mustangs are also driven by some teams in the National Hot Rod Association, or NHRA. Hot rods are cars that are rebuilt or changed to be faster. The NHRA is a drag-racing organization. Drag racing is different from NASCAR. In NASCAR races, cars are raced in a circle. In drag racing, cars race in a straight line. Mustangs also race in Grand-Am races. Grand-Am Road Racing races take place in North America.

First Generation

Ford divides its Mustangs into **generations**. The first generation of Mustang was made from 1964 until 1973. The first model of Mustang made was called the 1964½. Like all the Mustangs that followed it, the 1964½ had many different options. It could have either a V6 or V8 engine. It could have 105 **horsepower**, 164 horsepower, 210 horsepower, or 271 horsepower. The 1964½ could have a three-speed or four-speed manual **transmission**. The Mustang even had options for its roof. It could have a hardtop or a convertible top.

Here is a 1966 Mustang at a classic car show in 2010.

16

1967 Mustang

Engine size	6.4 liters
Number of cylinders	6 or 8
Transmission	Manual (stick shift)
Gearbox	5 speeds
0–60 mph (0–97 km/h)	7.4 seconds
Top speed	115 mph (185 km/h)

The 1970 Mustang Boss had a V8 engine.

In 1967, Ford redesigned the Mustang. It did this because other car companies were now making their own pony cars. The 1967 Mustang was bigger than earlier models. It could go up to 115 miles per hour (185 km/h) and had 320 horsepower. It could go from 0 to 60 miles per hour (0–97 km/h) in just 7.4 seconds!

Second Generation

The second generation of the Mustang, sometimes called Mustang II, began in 1974 and ended in 1978. The Mustang II was smaller and less powerful than the first generation. The first model of the second generation did not offer a V8 engine as an option. This disappointed Mustang lovers, but the car was still very popular. In 1975, Ford answered popular demand and began offering the option of a V8 engine. However, the Mustang still did not have the option for a convertible top, as the previous generation did.

This is the back end of a second-generation Mustang coupe.

1974 Mustang II

Engine size	2.3 or 2.8 liters
Number of cylinders	4 or 6
Transmission	Manual or automatic
Gearbox	4 speeds (manual) or 3 speeds (automatic)
0–60 mph (0–97 km/h)	13.8 seconds
Top speed	99 mph (159 km/h)

This is the front end of a second-generation Mustang coupe.

The 1974 Ford Mustang II had the option of either a V6 engine or a four-cylinder engine. The engine also came in two sizes, 2.3 liters or 2.8 liters. Because the Mustang II was less powerful than previous models, it had a top speed of only 99 miles per hour (159 km/h). It was available only as a **hatchback** or a **coupe**.

Third Generation

The third generation of Mustangs was made from 1979 until 1993. The 1979 Mustang was redesigned to look more like European sports cars. The body of the car was longer and taller, but it was lighter than earlier Mustang models. In 1984, Ford introduced the Mustang SVO. The SVO was a special-edition model. Only 4,508 SVOs were produced.

The SVO was powerful. It had 175 horsepower. The SVO was fast, too. It had a top speed of almost 135 miles per hour (217 km/h), and it could go from 0 to 60 miles per hour

Here is a 1979 Mustang 302. This year's model had the powerful Ford Windsor engine.

Mustang SVO

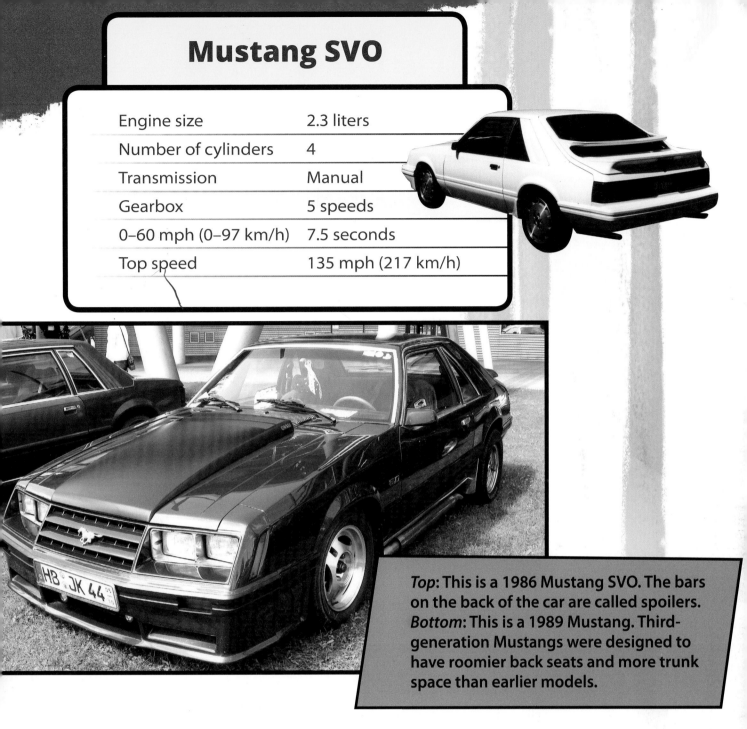

Engine size	2.3 liters
Number of cylinders	4
Transmission	Manual
Gearbox	5 speeds
0–60 mph (0–97 km/h)	7.5 seconds
Top speed	135 mph (217 km/h)

Top: This is a 1986 Mustang SVO. The bars on the back of the car are called spoilers. *Bottom*: This is a 1989 Mustang. Third-generation Mustangs were designed to have roomier back seats and more trunk space than earlier models.

(0–97 km/h) in just 7.5 seconds. At the time, it was the fastest Mustang available. The SVO had an I4 engine. These engines form a line, unlike V engines, which are shaped like a V. The SVO was highly thought of. However, it was the most expensive Mustang ever made, and because of this, it did not sell very well.

Fourth Generation

The thirtieth anniversary of the Mustang was celebrated in 1994. That year also marked the beginning of the fourth generation of the Mustang, which lasted until 2004. The fourth generation saw a major change in the design of the Mustang. Ford got rid of the hatchback option but continued to offer convertibles and coupes. Coupes are two-door sports cars. The fourth generation came at a difficult time for the Mustang. Sport-utility vehicles, or SUVs, were becoming more and more popular. Their

This is the concept version of the last of the fourth-generation Mustangs. A concept car is shown at auto shows before a model is produced for sale.

2004 Mustang GT Convertible

Engine size	4.6 liters
Number of cylinders	8
Transmission	Manual
Gearbox	5 speeds
0–60 mph (0–97 km/h)	6.3 seconds
Top speed	144 mph (232 km/h)

Here is the 1999 Anniversary Edition Ford Mustang convertible. This edition honored the Mustang's thirty-fifth anniversary.

popularity led to a decline in sales for the Mustang. Many other American carmakers stopped making sports cars, but Ford continued to make Mustangs.

In 2004, the Mustang turned 40. That same year, Ford produced its 300-millionth car, which was a Mustang GT convertible. A GT is a grand tourer. Grand tourers are luxury cars made for long-distance drives. The Mustang GT convertible had 260 horsepower and a V8 engine.

Fifth Generation

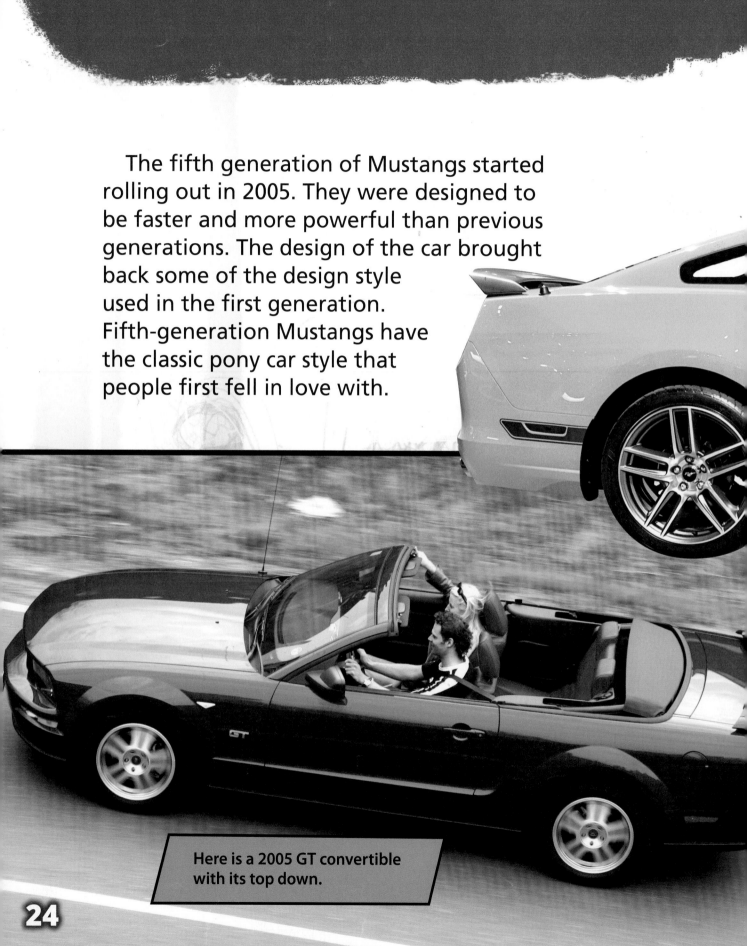

The fifth generation of Mustangs started rolling out in 2005. They were designed to be faster and more powerful than previous generations. The design of the car brought back some of the design style used in the first generation. Fifth-generation Mustangs have the classic pony car style that people first fell in love with.

Here is a 2005 GT convertible with its top down.

2012 Boss 302

Engine size	5.0 liters
Number of cylinders	8
Transmission	Manual
Gearbox	6 speeds
0–60 mph (0–97 km/h)	4 seconds
Top speed	155 mph (249 km/h)

The 2013 Mustang Boss 302 Laguna Seca takes its inspiration from racecars. It has a stiff suspension that lets the driver feel the road.

In 2011, Ford introduced the Mustang Boss 302. The original Mustang Boss was made in 1979 and 1980. The 2012 Boss 302 has a V8 engine and 380 pounds-feet of **torque**. It has 444 horsepower. The Boss is also very fast. It can go from 0 to 60 miles per hour (0–97 km/h) in 4 seconds and has a top speed of 155 miles per hour (249 km/h). The look of the Boss is inspired by racecars. It is low to the ground and very **aerodynamic**.

Racing Mustangs

In 2008, Ford introduced the Mustang Cobra Jet drag car. This Cobra Jet is a turnkey racecar. The car was introduced on the fortieth anniversary of the original Cobra Jet Mustang. The 2008 Cobra Jet is part of a series of racing Mustangs called FR500 and is also called FR500CJ. It is a very powerful car with 400 horsepower and a V8 engine.

Ford will be coming out with an even newer version of the Cobra Jet in 2013. Only 50 of the 2013 Cobra Jets will be made. The 2013 Mustang Boss 302S is one of Ford's newest racecars. It is based on the fifth-generation Mustang and has a V8 engine and 440 horsepower. It is made to be light and aerodynamic to help it go as fast as possible.

This racing Mustang is showing off its power at a motor show in Bologna, Italy.

2013 Boss 302S

Engine size	5.0 liters
Number of cylinders	8
Transmission	Manual
Gearbox	6 speeds

Mustangs Forever

Mustangs are still one of the most popular American sports cars. There were 11 different models of Mustangs made in 2012. They are the V6, V6 Premium, V6 Convertible, GT, V6 Premium Convertible, GT Premium, GT Premium Convertible, Boss 302, Shelby GT500, and Shelby GT500 Convertible. That may seem like a lot of options, but there are actually even more! Once you pick which model you want, you then pick the color, roof

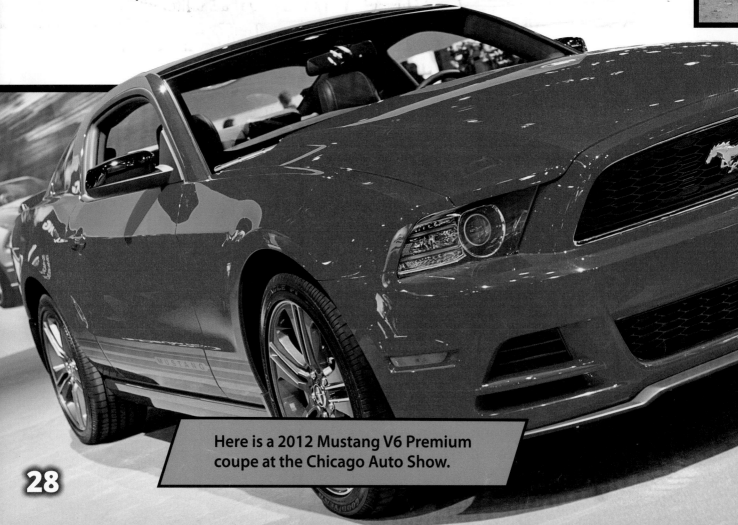

Here is a 2012 Mustang V6 Premium coupe at the Chicago Auto Show.

This 2011 Mustang GT has a 5.0-liter V8 engine and 412 horsepower.

type, grille, hood, headlights, and much more. People like having all of these options because they get to make their Mustangs exactly how they want them.

Mustangs will continue to be popular because they are American-made sports cars that are reasonably priced. Mustangs began as innovators and will continue to wow drivers into the future.

Comparing Mustangs

CAR	YEARS MADE	SALES	TOP SPEED	FACT
1967 Mustang	1967	472,121	115 mph (185 km/h)	This was the first convertible that had glass panes.
1974 Mustang II	1974	385,993	99 mph (159 km/h)	This generation changed its logo from a galloping mustang to a trotting mustang.
Mustang SVO	1984–1986	9,842	135 mph (217 km/h)	The SVO was the best-handling Mustang of third-generation Mustangs.
2004 Mustang GT	2004	1,896	144 mph (232 km/h)	The 2004 Mustang had the option of a red paint job with metallic racing stripes.
2012 Boss 302	2012	3,250	155 mph (249 km/h)	The Boss 302 Laguna Seca is named for a racetrack in California.

Glossary

aerodynamic (er-oh-dy-NA-mik) Made to move through the air easily.

affordable (uh-FOR-duh-bul) Low enough in price to be bought by many people.

assembly line (uh-SEM-blee LYN) A system in which a product is made by being moved down a line of workers and machines that complete different steps.

championships (CHAM-pee-un-ships) Contests held to determine the best, or the winner.

coupe (KOOP) A kind of car with two doors and a hard roof.

customizable (kus-tuh-MY-zuh-bel) Can be made or changed to suit a certain person.

cylinders (SIH-len-derz) The enclosed spaces for pistons in engines.

engineering (en-juh-NEER-ing) Making or using technology to create something.

generations (jeh-nuh-RAY-shunz) Things made during the same period.

hatchback (HACH-bak) A car with a back that opens upward.

horsepower (HORS-pow-er) The way an engine's power is measured. One horsepower is the power to lift 550 pounds (250 kg) 1 foot (.3 m) in 1 second.

innovative (IH-nuh-vay-tiv) Having new things.

manufactured (man-yuh-FAK-cherd) Made something by hand or with a machine.

torque (TORK) The force from a car's engine that produces rotation in the drive shaft.

transmission (trans-MIH-shun) A group of parts that includes the gears for changing speeds and that conveys the power from the engine to the machine's rear wheels.

turnkey (TURN-kee) Sold complete and ready to be driven.

Index

Websites

Due to the changing nature of Internet links, PowerKids Press has
developed an online list of websites related to the subject of this book.
This site is updated regularly. Please use this link to access the list:
www.powerkidslinks.com/smach/must/